MW01116147

LETTERS CALLED LIFE

by

Bryant Brewer

Bloomington, IN Milton Keynes, UK

authorHOUSE®

AuthorHouse™
1663 Liberty Drive, Suite 200
Bloomington, IN 47403
www.authorhouse.com
Phone: 1-800-839-8640

AuthorHouse™ UK Ltd.
500 Avebury Boulevard
Central Milton Keynes, MK9 2BE
www.authorhouse.co.uk
Phone: 08001974150

First published by AuthorHouse 5/31/2007

ISBN: 978-1-4343-1129-0 (e)
ISBN: 978-1-4343-1130-6 (sc)

Library of Congress Control Number: 2007903059

Printed in the United States of America
Bloomington, Indiana

This book is printed on acid-free paper.

Category 1

Category II:

Category III

LOVE PEACE OR DESTRUCTION

Category IV

Heaven And Earth

I raced through the galaxy
with rockets on high.

To my amazement I could truly
fly, without wings.

The stars streamed by at speeds unknown
to man, could this have been my master
plan, traveling without a craft.

Destination unknown, my speed
increased as the seconds ticked off.

Far off, yet rapidly approaching, a
bright light warmed my body.

I found myself being sucked into
an aura of sheer delight.

Suddenly the light began to dissipate
as I slowed to my final decent.

I witnessed a field of grass adorned with lilies
colored from the rainbow which halloed above.

Blue skies and the whitest clouds
presented the perfect backdrop.

Millions of bright, smiling faces
approached me from a rise in the
distance, and I became assured that
heaven could not be found on earth.

Myself On High

Blessed are the children born to my life.

Now with them everything is right.

I have given all that is contained in my mind.

They make me proud all of the time.

I look in their faces and see myself on high.

Oh! How my world begins to fly.

To feel the love which comes from their hearts.

They make me laugh with their brilliant smarts.

To you my children have no fear.

For yours truly, dad, will always be here.

To comfort, to love, to advise, to cry, and
fly with you down the path of your lives.

For every corner you turn, I'll be
there for your strength.

Mothers Song

You my Stef, could never be among the rest.

I gave you the greatest gift...Life.

Days have come and days have gone.

Know that I could never get
along...Without your love.

It seems as though we will be miles apart.

Rest assured you're in my heart...Forever.

Let it be known no matter where we are.

It will never be that far...Just call me.

No matter what you have heard my dear.

Make your own judgements and have
no fear...For mother loves you.

As sure as the sun shines.

We shall someday find our
selves together forever.

Living life as it was meant to
be from the beginning.

Letting go is the true test of our love.

Always remember my love...Mommy.

The Gift

I've have seen you life after life.

Our never-ending story travels on and on.

Not knowing calendar time, angels drawn
to each other never finding the last time.

Just beginning over and over again.

Strengthening what began centuries ago, I look
into your eyes, finding myself inside of you.

The blend of spirits so unmistakingly real.

I could never resist your touch.

It is unknown to me, yet so familiar.

Your words are more than just words.

They silhouette my earthly flesh.

Holding you in my arms, nothing more,
would complete my circle of tears.

Knowing I have come far aloft to be with you.

Take time to realize what you
should already know.

Missing you has become part of
the process of loving you.

Never fear the feelings of your soul.

They are pure and precise...
trust your gift from God.

Nothing More   NOTHING MORE

Life is but a mere blink in time and space.

We come and then we go.

Never knowing if we have done things right.

Most of our time spent trying
to extend time itself.

When it's all said and done.

The things accomplished to that
point are exactly what were meant to
occur without anything further.

Home

Moon struck by the blend of cascaded colors
of orange, red, yellow, and brown and even
the hint of black envelopes the desert floor.

All softly placed in this pastel setting, I
race to involve myself with its beauty.

Frequent stops are necessary. Hard, rugged
mountains rise up from the floor presenting
the perfect backdrop for the baron land
enriched with a multitude of life.

Day spent becoming part of what
eludes most that explore the floor
not realizing it's true beauty.

The single chirp of a hawk, the smell
of a wild pig makes me aware of the
simplicity of Gods creation.

The spirit exits the flesh and combines
with nature to create the world.

To become one with yourself, you
must become one with the creation
which lies beneath your feet.

The Resting Place

As the sun broke the cool of the
morning air my journey began.

Out of the sky came a rush of heat.

The birds sang with splendid
pleasure of the new day.

Nature became the conquest.

Briskly walking to find that nook in the
planet that could be all mine for just a
few hours to let my thoughts run wild.

I came to a hollow on the bank of a
river, which invited my company.

I sat and began to review.

The past blended correctly into the future.

A total calm came over my body.

I slumped into the soft pad of grass,
letting my emotions take over...bliss.

Dreamer

Night sets beyond the stars.

Lights shinning bright.

Feelings we posses in our
spirits become involved.

The moon glistens, it feeds our fantasy
of what each of us feels life should be.

Dreaming of a world with true perfection
which never materializes.

It just goes on and on.

Shall we ever find what is real
in our eyes, I think not.

Although the fun is in searching, never finding.

EDGE OF NATURE

I sit by the river edge.

A forest covered hill slopes
downward to its banks.

Sun shinning bright, no clouds to be found.

The warmth of it's rays, I
have longed all winter.

I have traveled hours for this
single spot of spring.

The foliage has yet to bloom.

I can hear the buds pushing and
struggling to reach the light of day.

Knowing it won't be long; I revel
in the sunshine for this time.

The beginning of many days
of nature is upon us.

A time for all life forms to awaken and
begin the work of revitalizing the planet.

The leaves will fall no more.

The time has come to grow.

Mankind will grow as well if he could
understand the warnings of nature, and
become a part of what he is made of...nature.

Have no fear of father leaving.

Even when I go, I take you with me.

All days are contained with thoughts of you.

Waiting for that time when I
come to you or you to me.

Our locations may be different, but
our homes are always the same.

There will always be a special
place prepared for you.

Let us never forget our love.

Someday you will understand why
adults do the things they do.

We say we love, yet hurt those
that listen to the words.

Life will continue with hurt and pain.

Its how we grow and prepare
for everlasting life.

Your destiny has already been mapped
out for you, and I am a part forever.

My love and wisdom runs through your veins.

When you need to see me, look in any
mirror and I'll be they're smiling.

Bryant To Bryant

In you I see my own life running wild yet
always knowing where it's headed.

Body so strong, lean, almost machine like.

Creative beyond belief, you
master all that you touch.

Not much for conversation yet your love
and wisdom always shines through.

Something's you have already
conquered, I once dreamed of.

It seems as though somehow my
life has been to its peak and now I
begin to live through you my son.

You have given me new joy and happiness.

Know that in all that you do I am with you.

I could never ask for more, for
you have given me all.

Stay as you are and continue to excel for
God has touched you with his own hands.

Love is a simple word for the
bond that we share.

Wish for the stars, there yours for the asking.

Bound For Death

Coast to coast I see the most
trying times of my life.

The earth splitting apart, we must
all pay for the sins of others.

On the other side, a frozen tundra.
Have we committed ourselves to
destruction according to his word?

Men having men, women having
women. Brothers kill brothers.

They're putting death up their noses.

A place where children are no longer children.

Wars rages out of control across the
planet. What are we all dying for?

The skies grow dark, and the fire
turns dark back into light.

Although the light has not come from
the source, we hoped it would.

The animal called, "disease", feeds on
millions of human body's year by year.

All things must come to pass.

Can we be moving through a
prophecy bound for death?

The planet lives. We live because of it's life, yet we poison it everyday with our technology, eventually causing our death.

He's on his return, prepare yourself, or you shall help replenish the earth.

Planet Survival

Lord, you are a powerful father; I give thanks
for life and the blessings you have given me.

To live in this world with such turmoil, my
soul boils with the pains of my existence.

A child of yours, living on, not in
this world. I make you the priority of
the day to sustain my survival.

My security lies within your hands. For your
son made the ultimate stand for us all.

Pardon sins.

Darkness engulfed my life, as
the love grew stronger.

I see your life manifest itself
from your mother's womb.

Never learning to love or care for
another life except your own.

Selfish, a word too meek to explain
the devils holds on your spirit.

Two masters you try to serve, bringing
down everyone around you.

Body contaminated with sores and sickness,
you revel in what you think as beauty.

The beauty exists only in the outer
crust of a non-existent soul.

You smell of rotting bowls,
longing to be cut out.

I fight the demons rushing from your mouth.

My faith must be and remain strong
to overcome your wrath.

No war is greater than the one I fight
with you, yet I tell you serpent.

You have been recognized and my faith and strength from God will command you from my life.

In Jesus name, Amen.

In The Beginning

Demanding our undivided attention.
Their colors are that of a rainbow.

They all thrive for the same things in life.

Born unknowing fear, segregation, or the
mean streaks evolved through time.

They have to experience horrible teachings
that time and their parents burden them with.

If only to remain young and innocent.

The world would surely be
one nation under God.

Save the children.

The blue grass of home shines ever so brightly.

Making stardust arise from the
hearts of all men alike.

I can only guess how frightening it
must be to have never experienced
a splendor such as this.

The mind must be open to whatever
comes from the soul of man.

Ready to fall into the deepest
caverns of the inner being.

Thrusting thoughts in and out
of ones consciousness.

Trying hard to avoid the comatose
state, never knowing if I could return
to what's thought of as reality.

Is your reality my reality, or could
this also be ones state of mine.

What I perceive as real, might
be fantasy in your mind?

Does that make my thoughts unwarranted?

Maybe our environments create
the reality around us.

THE NEW LIFE

The final stage of departure has come near.

My thoughts of ever lasting bliss is upon me.

A new life will be starting for the old.

Skies sprinkled with only clouds of joy.

I'm sure my vehicle will melt into the
seemingly never-ending road, which will
be traveled to the final destination.

The new life.

Life Form

I delve into life on the basis of give and take.

Remembering not to consume more
than what's needed to survive.

Knowing to use, yet not to abuse
the planet given by the father.

The earth will go on living as a breathing
mass extending from its liquid fire
core to the planet surface.

It overflows with life forms of all kinds.

Realize that we shall all become part of
its crust at the beginning of eternal life.

Remember to be kind to the living planet in
which you shall surely become part of.

I'll Come And Get You

AS I WALK ALONG THE LONELY
STREETS, I NEED TO SEE YOU AGAIN.

I NEVER THOUGHT I WOULD
NEED YOU SO BAD.

LET ME BE YOUR FRIEND.

ON THE DAY THAT YOU LEFT ME, I DID NOT
REALIZE THAT MY HEART WAS STILL YOURS.

I HAD TO FANTASIZE.

I KNOW THAT YOU'RE REALLY GONE,
AND YOU MAY NEVER COME AGAIN.

WHAT WILL I DO IF I NEVER SEE HER AGAIN?

IM FEELING SAD AND BLUE FOR YOU.

I WONDER IF SHE FEELS THE THINGS I
DO, OR HAS SHE THROWN ME AWAY.

IF GIVEN A CHANCE I WOULD
LIKE TO TRY AGAIN.

I'LL COME AND GET YOU TODAY.

Summers Dream

As I sat day dreaming, the phone rang.

The voice on the other end said, " hey man she really wants to meet you, how about tonight".

I replied with gleam, I'll come to your house after work, make sure she is there. The hours seemed like days.

I waited for work to end and meet what was to be my dream date.

On the drive to his house, I went over in my mind all the things I would say to this woman.

Finally I was there. I knocked and the door opened.

My friend was in the doorway, yet I never saw him.

From across the room her eyes came into contact with mine.

I knew she was pleased. The feeling was a mutual one.

Big brown eyes nestled into the cutest face I had ever seen.

I new this was pay dirt, but could we connect with any common interest.

I went to her for the introduction, and she
responded with a deep southern accent, which
traveled quickly to the depths of my heart.

Having gotten pass the awkward minutes of
surprise, we talked and talked and talked.

After an hour or more of conversation
we both knew this was the beginning
of something that could last.

Suddenly the phone rang and to
my amazement, I was awakened
from a deep sleep.
It was my friend. I said to him, " man I
just had the greatest dream of my life".

He replied, " no man, your dream just
got here, come over right now".

On And On

As we lock into our total embrace, your eyes
let me know I'm yours without question.

I must acquisition your final commitment.

As we kiss I swallow your breath
and gain fresh life within.

Soon I will go inside to combine.

The meat will swell and quench your hunger.

You fill, yet beg for more.

You are given what you need,
trembling I explode.

Feasting has been completed,
now you must rest.

I feel that I must go on.

There's much more that needs to be tasted

Your lips are moist, and I must taste
what has been left behind.

You try to push me away from your table,
but I hold tighter as I lick your bowl.

I knew this would return your
hunger, now your ready.

Once again inside, you tell me I belong, stay.

On and on we can go on and on.

No Logic In Love

Love has been master minded by some of the
best throughout time and yet none have found
true meaning or logic in what love continues
to make people of all walks do to themselves.

When you love you give more than love.

You give your will to correctly rationalize
or make sound decisions.

You tend to give away or throw away all that
you have previously worked so hard to sustain.

You have sight but become
blind to so many things.

Distortion becomes your way of life, never
benefiting your main purpose for existing.

A puppet, yet your strings can not be found.

Sleepless nights and jealous
accusation, where is the logic.

Maybe it's not the logic. It's the feeling,
or nature's animal instinct to make
sure the species will survive.

Logic and the mind might be
why love can't be logical.

Emotions and logic mix probably
as well as oil and water.

There could never be a correct formula for love.

Give way and let love control itself.

When It's Time To Break

I picked up the telephone and
dialed those seven digits.

The hardest call I have ever attempted.

Just as I feared, the busy signal was present.

Call after call, I could not get through.

A vision that came to me nights
before, keeps me awake.

I had to complete this or sleep
would never come.

She had me right where she wanted me,
hanging dangerously from the cliffs of love.

Could I find strength to endure?

I wonder aimlessly about the house
waiting to complete the call.

Heart pounding, mind racing,
It's time to try again.

I must gather my thoughts.

To my discuss, it was still busy.

The outcome is already set.

Controlling, she is the master.

Shall we ever learn the game, or just
keep plying with fear and pain.

Step By Step

STEP BY STEP

As you travel sifting through the lives
of others, your heart grows larger,
because of the caring attitudes you
take with every step placed forward.

Knowing you could never turn from
the destiny set out for you.

Acceptance of your mission has
been long since accomplished.

Life spent comforting, caring, helping;
loving and giving all that is in you,
offered without question.

Just your presence creates an atmosphere
of total calm and cohesion.

Always give what's been given to you.

Your power is faith and love for mankind.

Forever remain as you are, for you
and I am traveling two parallel
roads, which will meet in time.

It's our destiny.

Simplicity

A value greater than all the gold held
by the riches of all civilizations.

This is why you are that special diamond
gem coiled around my fibers.

Your love for the simple things of life runs
parallel to existence with the father above.

The phrase," keep it simple stupid", is always
there for me to bring to the front on my
mind when I start to complicate things.

We have managed to keep ourselves
basic in our needs of each other.

This has created in my mind an irresistible
urge to share my wildest and deepest
thoughts and secrets with you.

It has come to pass that without you I'm a mere
shell or fragment of the person your helping to
potentially create. I know now, you're the one.

DESTINY SOUL TO SOUL

You always seem to bring something out
in me, which is usually undiscovered and
somehow raw until you touch me with
whatever it is that you touch me with.

A true friend you are, and I cherish each
and every moment I have with you,
however insignificant it may be.

I have found a strange yet
wonderful love in you.

I will always be there for you.

I'm just sad that we could not have met under
different circumstances in a different time.

I could truly be yours for a lifetime.

Attraction comes strongly to your intellect.

We often debate, no subject excluded.

At times I find myself knowing your thoughts
without words ever being exchanged.

Total package, would surely
explain your essence.

Your physical beauty surrounds
the caring, loving, and generous
attributes held within your shell.

I shall wait for you. I know you will come
to me, because it is meant to be.

Our connection and love will surely come to
pass with time for I have seen the future.

Pure Appreciation　　　PURE APPRECIATION

Crystals of water fell from the sky, blanketing
the rolling hills, brought magic to my eyes.

White as cotton balls as far as the eye can see.

Winter tragically on us, you run
rapidly through my mind.

I must tend the fire, for your warmth
remains my only desire.

Without you, I am still with you.

You are mine to understand, unlike the
snowflake, complex, although reachable.

It shall someday melt away, yet you
always remain covertly for my heart.

I sit staring with expectations on
high, as the snow races pass me.

The storm has become one of comfort. It brings
back days past of love, joy and wonderment.

To share this long lost miracle from
God with you has created one of many
memories I will forever cherish.

Your honesty has been as pure as the
snowflake, so white and clean.

Note my appreciation.

Fifty Fifty

Sunshine, blue skies, the rain
has come to my life again.

Why is true love so hard to find?

The more you give translates to
more being taken away.

Could there really be a 50-50 love,
out there, somewhere.

I've always felt that we should
give all that we have.

Nine times out of ten you will
be treated like a rag.

The players always change, but
the game remains the same.

Will You Come

You have captured my heart with
the grace of your smile.

I have come to know the simple
and wild... nature within you.

All your thoughts are so fresh and clean.

I could not imagine you being mean.

You say there is no black or white in your life.

I'll have to concur, and say that's nice.

To know you has become my life torn dream.

I feel as part of a special team with you.

At times I sit and stare into space.

With you on my mind that's amazing grace.

Believe my words are sincere, there's
truly nothing for you to fear.

The connection has been sealed, and it's
loud and clear, my world is yours my dear.

loves creed

I long for love to entice and share my dreams.

I need that love to build esteem.

Life without love is not life at all.

Just a mere existence rooted
with everyday routines.

We search and we search without an end,
hoping to find that magical blend called love.

Are we ever really sure if it's real and true,
or just a fascination for ones own greed?

If you take, expect to give. Within
this realm the love will live.

Be not selfish.

Communicate freely as often as you can,
yet allow that space which invades us.

Touch with affection, and be
emotional from your heart.

Become one single part.

In love, two should equal one.

The Take Over

My heart peaks with the mystical
magic of your love.

I tend to sore as the doves, with you in mind.

Common place no longer appears to be real.

The fantasy has taken over
my mainstream of life.

At some point the fantasy will
create a triumphant co-existence
with spirit and mortality.

Dipping in and out of reality.

Knowing full well that my reality is
becoming my own state of mind.

This gives me the advantage to place myself
in any situation for my own pleasures.

Everything shall surely become
what ever I wish it to become.

Darlene Queen

Girl you have become my queen,
the dear and only Darlene.

Your eyes, they sparkle so bright, capturing my
heart more and more with your every glance.

You have become my never-ending dream.

Showering my thoughts and then
leaving me breathless.

Close to losing you my eyes were opened
with the realization that you are the
one sent from the heavens above.

You will surely be cherished, loved,
and honored for the kindness that you
exude to everyone in your presence.

I vow to spend my life keeping you secure, and
filled with the happiness of my love for you.

I am now and forever yours exclusively,
wanting for nothing less than what
only you, Darlene can provide.

My thoughts run wild when thinking
of you, and your magical aura.

There is a glow that envelops your
presence whenever I am near you.

Can I touch your sunset?

It radiates warmth from you soul.

You are blessed with the soul
of God's own hand.

I have looked through the windows of your
soul to find my deepest desires, which
I express with little or no regrets.

My expressions have been but a mere
grain of sand lost on a beach, which
stretches into and beyond eternity.

You my friend have rekindled a passion
within me I feared had left forever.

You have given me strength to wonder
my mind, gather fresh thoughts, and want
for more than the practical and safe.

To delve into adventure, I find
excitement when living on the edge.

Do what you feel you should do, not
what you wish you could have done.

My new lease comes from your strength.

Your love is love.

First Mothers Love

Like a new child fresh from the womb.

This day has meaning far greater
than all could imagine.

For birth comes in many ways.

Each being special in it's own way.

This matter brings forth the birth of
a new and meaningful relationship,
which will stand the test of time.

God has made it so.

Let it be known that love abounds
your very existence, being witnessed
by all that surrounds you.

A mother's love is greater than love itself.

You always let your love spill over all mankinds.

On this day I commit to you
my ever-lasting love.

Robbins

As a Robin of the night, you called to me.

"Yes", I hear your call.

I have seen the light of your smile.

Can this be the trial, for your love?

Knowing the struggle may be long.

You have warranted me for the challenge.

You have brought me into your covenant.

I have learned the longing of your heart.

Our co-existence runs parallel.

I have seen in you all that I am.

We shall fly unrestricted through the night.

It will surely become right if we continue.

Love Being Happiness

Accused of things never taking place.

Near insanity with love, I have loss something,
which has captured my every fiber.

I know she has created situations, and lodged
accusations because of her fear and deep
hidden want to extinguish the relationship.

I find myself suffering from pain and
anguish she has accumulated from
past relationships and love affairs.

I accepted the abuse with hopes
that someday it would dissipate
leaving us to live happy together.

To be accused of wrong doings or
simply being ignored tends to develop
traits of pain and suffering which no
human should be subjected to.

I will and have loved this woman.

The time has come for her to take that
journey to find mainly herself which will bring
contentment and her needed peace of mind.

Someday you will realize the extent of my
love and how some wrongs in your eyes were
actually rights that you just could not see.

I wish only the best for you.

I will pray that you find the happiness
that I could not provide.

It was all yours.

Love being happiness.

Love Traits

In the flesh you're not her, all though
in my heart you remain forever.

Many tell me to let go, but that's impossible.

We have gone together from riches
to rags, then back to riches.

In and out of hard times, yet always
remaining side by side.

How can one let go of what makes
him inhale the breath of their life.

What make them feel what they never felt?

That being their ultimate loves.

You shall keep me and I shall keep you.

Always knowing the pains and
pleasures that only we know and
have experienced being together.

Our tears and joys have melted
the sands of the desert.

Our feet have tread over mountains so high.

The love has never faltered.

Someday the union created under
the heavens will overflow again and
on through our eternal lives.

Come back to our future.

Touch

The moon came up over the horizon.

The calm of the night fell over the earth.

All movement somehow became still.

I reached for the twinkling stars above.

A rush of cool air swept across my bare chest.

I knew this would be a night to remember.

Then suddenly I heard the crackling
of twigs, and leaves under foot.

I looked to my right, and there
she lies beside me.

Her eyes pierced the innermost
parts of my spirit.

We interlocked our bodies, and soared
through the darkness of night to eternity.

Selfish Reality

Magical thoughts of love, and my
consciousness slips from reality.

Mind set no longer existent.

The fantasy must take over.

On to the place were all becomes possible.

I shall create my bliss without
hostility or resistance.

You dear, are whom ever I wish you to be.

Striving for my personal happiness only.

The System

THE SYSTEM

I met you through a communicative
electric system.

I was instantly swept away, and
your pulse connected tightly.

Your voice has become the funnel
for which I depend on sanity.

You my electric lady have created a storm
bellowing from the depths of my heart.

Can this possibly go on with nothing further?

Hours given to the connection of the bond.

Built firmly, not faltering under pressure.

Never having seen you inside,
I hunger for more.

Continually building the emergence
of our thought patterns.

They flow electronically from soul to soul.

How have we become to be so bold?

Using mans electric to spawn a
tantalizing blend of humanity.

Taking Me Over

As time passes, my mind becomes more
and more involved in the thought of you.

Your face, your voice, the smell of your
fragrance, the softness of your hair, the
beauty of your smile, and the overwhelming
desire to be with you has taken me over.

Whether you need me or not,
I am your eternally.

You may not know, but you have
given me so much happiness.

My life has become a new.

All the reasons to live are now present.

Waiting A Lifetime

You my dear have erased all of the
fear of knowing something new.

Someday I'll know what's in store for you and I.

You feel my thoughts when I am not even there.

You have found your way inside of me.

You do not control but can dictate my
actions, knowing the reaction.

Your heart being entangled in a web
of love, I still long to be with you.

For there is something uncontrollably
viable about what has been
created between you and I.

Waiting a lifetime could never be to long for
the true comfort of your constant love.

Somehow my wisdom assures me
that this shall come to pass.

Patients being on my side, I rest
contented during the journey of turmoil
which shall bring us together forever.

Stand by.

Down On Happiness

You have sparked me once again.

When I am down at the end of
happiness, you always appear.

How could I ever fear loosing you?

Your flesh could never over power the
soul I've come to know so well.

The bond has been set for the journey.

We travel unrestricted in our
thoughts, always knowing love.

Remember I have been committed,
whether together or not.

Some how I must stand fast to you.

The years have come and gone,
yet I am still there.

The struggle has to be worth the prize.

I will be waiting beside the still
waters for you, truly.

American Dream

Unrest in the streets, it surely
beat the brothers down.

You're not white so stay on your side of town.

Trying peacefully to gain the equality
that is rightfully theirs according to the
constitution of the United States.

Rallies on college campuses, marches in their
own communities, have all become shooting
galleries for the masses of authority.

The time had come to move
to the front of the bus.

There was a stand for all of us as a people.

Black and white alike new it was
right and the stage was set.

Ready to dye, there could be no retreat.

Brothers being killed in war came home
to be denied at the voting booths.

In whose hand does the justice lie?

Vietnam, most would never
again see their mom.

Kent State, how many made it to the gate.

JFK, he never saw the day
he once dreamed off.

Martin Luther, how many times must
he go to the mountaintop?

Why did so many die for the accomplishments
of the time, just to see the race split
and in total disarray in the nineties.

Come together my people for there
is so much work left to be done.

Think with your minds not your emotions.

Genesplicing

Bodies sleek and clean, like the rock
and sculpture to perfect forms.

Knowing how it responds, hours
are given to its creation.

Genetics where given to build on.

The genesis was in the mind, which quickly
took itself to the physical response,
nurtured by the thought pattern.

The proportions have come together
in the correct format.

Nothing being larger or smaller,
the mass is fluent.

Not easily achieved, you must
maintain with consistency.

Precise fueling must also take
place on regular intervals.

Once fueled, down time will take place for the
complicated rebuilding process required.

After years of commitment coupled
with desire and motivation, your
masterpiece shall be realized.

Where Have All The Leaders Gone

Where have all the leaders gone.

Crack rules the streets; we are at
the peak of human disaster.

Where have all the leaders gone,
babies having babies, they're crying
so loud, but we cannot hear them.

Where have all the leaders gone, guns
firing in the night, the blood of our
future runs cold in the streets.

Where have all the leaders gone,
there families are broken, the support
system becomes crips and bloods.

Can anyone tell me where the leaders are?

Where have all the leaders gone, jails
overflowing, brothers, your people
will never survive with you there.

Where have all the leaders gone, the
children are watching, yet you do not
give them the food they need.

Can anyone tell me where the leaders are?

The leaders need there people to
emerge; not one body can be whole
without each and every part.

We are all a part of our culture
body, come together so our leaders
can surface and guide us.

Backroads

They search by day for the sacrifice victim
for their night of what they think to be fun.

Victims usually black, young,
intelligent, and well spoken.

As a male he posses the greatest
threat to their culture.

Totally unwarranted, it's the fear in the beast.

They are adorned in white,
looking like cone heads.

They travel the back roads to find the
most secluded area to perform their
shameful and spineless rituals.

Since the conception of this so-
called free country, being minority,
Jewish, or of color appears to be a
crime in the eyes of the majority.

No credit ever given for their multitude of
contributions, their history totally erased.

They still struggle for their
place within society.

The media dramatizes their crimes, usually
against each other, yet never speaking of
the crimes the cone heads have committed
and continue to perpetrate as I speak.

They long to hold onto their slaving ways.

Their control is beginning to slip.

The covert war fought for years is being
lost and they know not what to do.

The races are slowly becoming one.

The cone heads cannot handle the realization
that even they are not pure anymore.

They will have to concede or perish.

Begin At The End

Minute by minute, constantly searching for
the next moment, can I go much further?

There must be a way to exploit the minutes
which grow into hours, which grow into
days, which grow into months, which grow
into years and on and on throughout time.

The circle becomes smaller as we grow
older, what is the meaning of it all.

Life seems to be many circle cycles, which
always return to their same absolute beginning.

Sometimes the circle is broken which
creates an entirely new circle.

Knowing your place in the circle
will help your cycle.

The speed with which you evolve will
determine the success and rewards
your circle shall grant to you.

The circle will give you only one full cycle, so
you must be on target and at the correct pace.

Remember the ending of your circle
cycle will be it's beginning as well.

Red Corvette

Metal gleaming in the sunshine, with
rubber soft as a baby's ass.

It called for me to mount its interior.

Smooth leather flowing, rising up and attached
to every possible crevice within the womb.

I so badly wanted to go inside to feel
and taste its inviting flavors.

It rumbled from the strength of its guts.

They were precisely measured
to its greatest potential.

It rocked towards me, and
begged for my assistance.

It took all I had to resist.

I knew its pitch was about to
reach climax proportions.

So I did what was necessary, I climbed
aboard the little red corvette, stood
on the floorboard, and drove into that
twelve-inch tree down the street.

Something's we may want so badly
might just come true, although they
could go in a split second.

Be patient, things have a way of coming
in there own time and space.

The Real Status

Does anyone ever really master anything
in life, personally I think not, although
that can be construed from my belief
in what mastering might be.

Can or do we as a people reach a
point that may be no more than we
can consume mentally, to master.

Or do we just go on learning and learning,
never reaching that climax as the flesh does.

That master may be to self actualize and
then there can be nothing further.

You have reach all that could
possibly be accomplished.

Who knows maybe this could be the cause
of spontaneous human combustion, and like
ground zero, you become the shadow?

So be careful on how and what you
may set out to achieve, you just might
take it to the next level, and find out its
somewhere you really did not want to be.

Once your there you cannot return.

You met the master yet there was
still more he needed to learn.

Can you strive for more and
still claim master status.

Lets Play Once Again LETS PLAY ONCE AGAIN

The game is set; the heroes adorn
their armor of plastic and steel.

They sit and study the opponent's
game plan, formulating the own.

Yet it will come down to sixty minutes
of play to achieve the out come, and
there can only be one triumphant.

The fans will be chanting, betting
and at some point taking the stadium
to a fever pitch of excitement.

At this point one of the teams will emerge
and take control of the game destiny.

Their strength is quite evident, and they
control both sides of the line, knowing
that soon the prize will belong to them.

Being so close they play even harder,
totally disregarding painful injuries to
complete their task which took close
to six months to have realized.

Realize yourself that men enjoy
playing kid games.

The stakes just become higher.

The Departure

A calm came over the usual active
tendencies of the household.

The children were silent.

Even the pets were still and subdued.

Wife drifted into a comatose state.

What could be wrong I wondered?

Have I walked into an unnatural
reflection of my own life style?

Maybe I had powered myself into a
future time not in existence yet.

Then again could it be an
unconscious wish for privacy.

To any extent, it was unwanted
and very disturbing.

Life without positive attitudes and
actions creating reactions couldn't
possibly be life as it was intended.

See No, Hear No

SEE NO HEAR NO

Time to travel and explore the unknown
distinction of what's unknown.

Nothing but space surrounds
everything that you must be.

Unaware of the most trivial things which
might or are about to be unveiled.

Like the snake, you have eyes but cannot see.

Slithering from rock to rock only to
be disappointed at every arrival.

Ears tightly secured to all that speak.

No where will you ever be.

**Machismo erupting from the fibers of muscle
contracting and expanding, assuring himself
the he is everything in his own mind.**

**He invites himself to the nearest available
mirror to explore what is not really there.**

Try to tell him that.

What has happened to the shivery of days old?

There has to be more to life than yourself.

**If you search for the answer, you will
find it above your shoulders.**

Behind The Walls

Revile is called and they exit their cells.

Begging for the breakfast, the
sandman still in their eyes.

The call is given and they race
to be first for the spoils.

They all return fat and happy at your expense.

It is now time to sleep away another day.

They live and breathe, but surely do not exist.

The sleep is needed to store energy
for the afternoon and night filled with
the deadly games they like to play.

No one is exempt or safe from the madness.

They awaken like devils of the night,
ready they begin the nightmare.

If this is the state of madness behind
the walls, just how safe do you feel
negotiating the civilian sector?

Commitment

They came with the smell of
alcohol on their breath.

The starry gaze in their eyes
from a night on the pipe.

Sometimes with railroad tracks adorning arms.

At this point authority posses
their largest problem.

Asking questions unable to be answered.

They physically lash out at
their own discuss within.

Then comes violent retaliation from authority.

Never admitting guilt from the night
of terror they left behind.

Victims bleeding, crying, and crawling
through the night's darkness searching
for comfort, which is rarely found.

You have finally found yourself in the place
where hopefully you shall remain, jail.

Affective Crime

Being taught from birth the differences
between right and wrong.

Some venture into the cruel and
calculated world of crime.

Always enjoying profit of their
pleasure until caught.

Then crying and begging for everyone's pity.

Always claiming to be a victim
of circumstances.

Fighting hard for every
constitutional right afforded.

Rights which should be stripped the minute
the gavel falls with the guilty verdict.

All of the granted rights and rehabilitative
measures have taken away any deterrent
that may have existed at all.

Can it be that we as a society have
forgotten who the real victims are?

The more modern the system
becomes the less affective it is.

Concrete, Steal And A Nine Mil

CONCRETE, STEEL AND A NINE MIL

Signs of the times are upon us,
lurking, quirking, and totally
destroying mans best endeavors.

Fires ragging, the planet surface
is splitting at the seams.

The sky grows darker with each passing year.

The seas are shrinking by and by.

The population swelling, no food to
eat, and no place to sleep cold enters
the body causing hardness.

The babies are crying.

Drugs run ramped causing the display
of weapons for destruction.

Death comes by the hundreds of thousands.

If I don't know you, then I must
shoot, killing you to eventually cause
my own subsequent death.

The cycle has taken control.

It's circumference rapidly decreasing,
we run with no where to hide.

The only hope lies in the hands of children.

Kid Games

Cap the pool of urban violence.

Warfare for the youth runs wild in the streets.

Knives shinning bright in the
moonlight of the night.

Guns being drawn, bullets strike
at any available target.

Something has been lost in days long gone.

Newscasters walk daily in the
blood of unknowing victims.

The script is usually a carbon
copy of the prior day.

Four dead from gun shot wounds, one stabbed
in robbery, and on till the viewers grow
horrid with discuss or fear of their own fait.

13, 14, 15, no longer teenage years.

We have created combat tested
soldiers in our urban communities.

The war is in full effect, and the
enemy is very hard to detect.

Will it take violence to stop violence, or
shall we keep treating teenage adults
as if they are to young to understand
the nature of their actions.

Not just kid games.

Pains Of War

As I walk through the valley the
shadows confuse the light.

Slowly moving into the darkness
of something unknown to me.

Fear takes over the soul.

That fear of the unknown has become the
greatest fear ever encountered by mankind.

Never knowing if you shall be taken by
surprise, you must move briskly.

Landscape begins to squeeze
as it encompasses you.

Noises of the night somehow begin to intensify.

You feel the vibration of their
pressure, yet you move on.

What could it be that compels you
to search so unrelentingly?

A rush of air steams by you,
scampering for cover, you wonder.

When the calm returns, again
you move, one by one.

Never really knowing if the body in front of you
is the correct one, you trust only with instinct.

It's hard to keep your silence, yet you know
its essential to your common mission.

Twelve of the best are with
you, but you are unsure.

Suddenly the night is lit, screams cry out,
bodies are hurled against the planet surface.

My chest begins to burn uncontrollably.
Warm liquid fills my hand as I grasp.

Knowing how and where this madness all
began, there's to little on me here to let it end.

The only end should be that of war. Man should
not have to endure its pain. Let there be peace.

Winter

The sun melted behind the horizon.

A leaf drifted slowly towards the ground.

In my amazement I noticed a cloud
emerge from the warmth of my breath.

Darkness engulfed the skies, but
not a cloud to be found.

My only escape was indoors.

There I found a fire raging.

Orange, red, and gold embers
raced up the chimney.

Could this be what I feared?

WINTER.

SWEET REDWOOD

The pine needles stick and prick, but I
long for the sap of sweet redwood.

Glistening in the summer sun,
nestled among the forest canopy, you
stand so tall, sweet redwood.

I hold you.

The pine needles stick and prick, but I
long for the sap of sweet redwood.

The moss flows from your
branches like a lion's main.

I have to reframe, for my love
is sweet redwood.

She reaches continually for the sky.

I long to be by and by with sweet redwood.

BY: BRYANT BREWER
COPY RIGHTS 2007